Alternative Poetry Books

This is the Yellow edition of my alternative poetry books series. There will be six more to come. To give you some idea of what to expect, here are quotes from some of my readers:

"I hate poetry with a vengeance, but banana's book is really funny. This is a book for haters of poetry. " Australia

"Poetry is about painting pictures in a few words that others need pages to do. Banana does that well, which is why it's good stuff. " USA

"Lovely, so refreshing and unpretentious." UK

"I'm laughing so much, I have a pain in my side. You are evil." South Africa

"Rather middle class and a trifle condescending, but luckily balanced by humour." Europe

So there you are. If you hate poetry you may well enjoy this. If you like poetry you might enjoy it too.

The 100,000+ people who visited my poetry4fun blog gave me the confidence to put this series together. To them and to you I'd like to say thank you very much – you give me purpose.

Coming soon from Endaxi Press...

The **Pink** edition of the Alternative Poetry Books

The **Blue** edition of the Alternative Poetry Books

The **Green** edition of the Alternative Poetry Books

The **Red** edition of the Alternative Poetry Books

The **Orange** edition of the Alternative Poetry Books

The **Purple** edition of the Alternative Poetry Books

but not necessarily in that order.

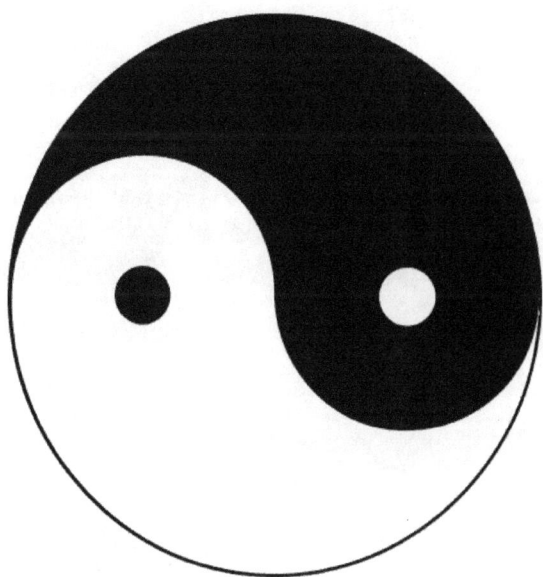

Alternative Poetry Books

Yellow edition

Michele Brenton
(banana the poet)

Endaxi Press

First Edition published 2009
by Endaxi Press
2nd Floor, 145-157 St John Street, London, EC1V 4PY

www.endaxipress.com

ISBN   978-1-907375-00-2

British Library Cataloguing in Publication Data.
A catalogue record for this book is available from the British Library.

Printed by Lightning Source, Kiln Farm, Milton Keynes.

The author may be contacted directly via:
http://poetry4fun.blog.co.uk

*Dedicated to
the memory of
my Papa - Marc Alter.*

I remember everything you taught me...

How this book is organised.

Poems which start on even numbered pages are intended to be 'serious' poems which I associate mainly with my 'real' persona - Michele Brenton.

Poems which start on odd numbered pages are intended to be 'funny' poems which I associate mainly with my web persona - banana the poet.

So if you feel like reading a frivolous quirky little something - start on an odd page.

If your mood is more earnest then try the poems on the even pages.

Alternative Poetry Books
Yellow edition
Contents

A Plea to Poetry Readers!	1
Cut Glass Floor	2
Tinkering with the ivories or why I'm not a dentist	3
Sincere apologies to my teacher	5
The Great Wall of China	6
Sharper than a serpent's tooth...	7
The Salvation of Disorganisation	8
A Taste of France? Non Mon Sewer!	9
Dust	10
What the music teacher really thinks	11
For Neda	12
Where there's dirt there's life	13
Thought Balloon	14
Little Jimmy and the Sweet Corn of Doom	15

In every breath as always potential for disaster 16

A Question of Pants!! 17

The Hero Party 18

Grown Ups 19

Papa's Poem 20

Entente Cordiale 21

Land of my Mothers 22

Mother and the Monkey 23

Mad Dog and Englishman 24

Tea-Pot of Trouble 25

I Quit 28

Dog Day Afternoon 29

Loss 30

The Person who said "Yes" to Spam 31

Lessons will be learned 32

A Prickly Problem	33
Poising I Be	34
Halfway round the bend	35
Torreilles	36
The World on its Head	37
A Couple of Haiku	38
Nu Labour Christmas Carol	39
De Problem with De-Fooing	41
Call me 'Home'	42
Happy Anniversary Darling	43
Here Today, Gone Tomorrow	44
Father's Day	45
Summer anticipated	46
Government Advice for Summer in the UK	47
Love or 'In love'?	48

Nonsense Poem   49

Suffer little children...   50

Warn Parenting   51

Carnaval   52

Cauliflower soup c'est delicieux   53

Ode to a Greek Taxi Driver   55

Finding home   56

Snooze and you lose   57

I took my love   58

Mr BadShock   59

Love all   60

My Funny Valentine   61

Now I've Grown   62

What's in a name?   63

The games you play   64

Money can't buy you love   65

Yellow   66

NEVER DO ...   67

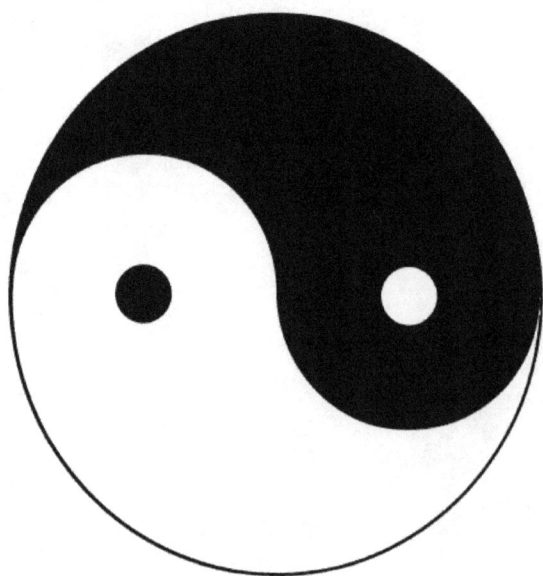

A Plea to Poetry Readers!

Why can't people say what they mean,
speaking clearly to listening ears?
Not intoning riddles pompously
and boring me to tears?

I like my poetry succinct.
Nicely put, but to the point.
I hate that flowery mannered stuff,
I yearn to scream and quit the joint.

So if by some unlikely twist,
this rhyme's to be read out of a book
read it simply without airs,
or risk being felled by my swift right hook.

Cut Glass Floor

Promises are brittle glass
lying shattered on the floor.
I walk on them with naked feet
whilst heading for the door.

The cuts are deep and bloody
I'm familiar with the pain.
Once I close that door behind me
I won't have to feel again.

You dance amongst your promises
an angry gypsy reel,
not noticing my drops of blood
staining your metal heels.

I cannot remain the enemy within
and the lover left without,
tormented by each devil mood,
diminished by each shout.

So I walk towards that open door
to some other universe.
Freed of my ancient fear of death
by living something worse.

Tinkering with the ivories – or why I'm not a dentist

When I was young and still a virgin
I studied to become a dental surgeon.
It was my earnest eager plan
to ease the pain of my fellow man.

I enjoyed the first year - mainly theory
but for human dissection which I found rather eerie.
The second year was my stumbling block
I'll tell you why, but please don't mock.

My nemesis turned up one day
a frail old lady – hair of grey.
Lisping softly she asked me 'Pleeth,
can I have thome new falth teeth?'

Many years had passed since her face had a tooth
her gums had receded along with her youth.
There was hardly a ridge left upon which to base
a new set of gnashers to furnish her face.

She needed techniques very complex and long
of the sort one would hope to be gloried in song.
So I rolled up my sleeves and engaged in the work
necessary to give her a shiny new smirk.

Many appointments came and went.
My back was to my object bent.
Each tiny adjustment was made with her nod
they had to be perfect as if made by God.

Tears and sweat and time were spilled.
At last the plastic gums were filled
with perfect porcelain works of art
placed and chosen with all my heart.

That her teeth weren't natural you couldn't tell.
As I gazed upon them my pride full swell
the daughter she'd brought for the very first time
poured forth her wisdom to opine.

'Oh Mum, I think they're a little too yellow!'
Says Mum 'Oh yes, what d'you think young fellow?'
I tried to remind her we'd chosen the hue
to go with her age – she was old and not new.

But the daughter held firm – she'd have gone on all night.
'If she's having new teeth – they ought to be white!'
Along came my tutor observing my pout,
held the teeth towards me and said 'Grind them out.'

'Use them as trays to take new impressions,
start all over again, book her in for more sessions.'
Instead of beginning all over again
I decided I was sick of my fellow men.

If they had pain – then that was tough.
Someone else could help them
I'd had enough.

For Fred Le Grand.

Sincere apologies to my teacher

I'm sorry I bit Mrs ThreadGold,
it's not a thing I'd do twice.
Quite apart from the fact that I won't get the chance,
she didn't taste very nice.

The Great Wall of China

From space you can see it
it's really that huge,
a structure of cosmic dimensions,
and yet it was built before JCB
or other earth moving pretensions.

These days we may feel
we cannot make change
with mankind pitted brother 'gainst brother.
But the Great Wall of China
shows what we can do
by just putting one brick on another.

For Dan Holloway.

Sharper than a serpent's tooth...

The night is over at long last.
Sun comes up as darkness fades.
I'm not refreshed from sleep alas
for I've been peeing razor blades.

Every hour on the hour
the call has come to pass
water I've been swigging down
which turns to shards of glass.

Despite taking medication
I'm sick and tired and sadder
from avoiding dessiccation
by flushing out my bladder.

There would be a prize indeed
for whoever would delight us
by finding how to rid the world
of horrible cystitis!

For Rebecca - my friend on Twitter.

The Salvation of Disorganisation

I have
an urge to
organise
ritualise
alphabetise
categorise
every damned thing.

I could
completely
lose self control
by being in
complete control
and sanitizing out the soul
of every damned thing.

I feel
the roll-call
anodyne
a need to put
myself in line.
A place for me and me in mine
like every damned thing.

A Taste of France? Non Mon Sewer!

Never miss a chance
to drive in Northern France
on the lovely roads marked N.
They were designed
with you in mind,
by understanding men.

The places through
which they take you
are beautiful and green
with gentle undulations
and many a sparkling stream.

And often as you
are driving through
a tiny French village
you are greeted
by yet another reason why
N's are better than payages.

The smell of food
from somewhere good
recommended by Les Routiers.
A place to rest
and taste the best
maybe from the local charcutier?

But please take heed
whatever your need
no matter how hungry you get.
Don't be led astray
whatever they say
Never try Andouillette!

And if you do you may well say
"Poo! That's something I'll never forget!"

Dust

Sun rises in the east,
  in that simple fact we trust,
light that gives us all we see
  and makes a dancer of the dust.

We will rise up in the sun,
  we will join it as we must,
light that holds us in its glow
  even after we are dust.

  Snow shines in the winter glare,
  ice melts in its rays.
  Trees grow, unfold their leaves.
  Birds glide in haze.

Sun shines on all who are,
  warms the sinner and the just,
light that colours in the days
  and makes a dancer of the dust.

For June and Frank.

What the music teacher really thinks

The devil makes work for idle hands;
thus the violin was born,
from whose tortured throat,
screaming notes are torn.

The world is full of wickedness
debauchery and sin.
So as a fitting punishment,
we have the violin.

For Neda

the sun shines.
still blue sky.
birds sing swoop and dive.

A shot rings out.

empty sky.
red stained ground.
yet the sun still shines.

R.I.P.

Where there's dirt there's life

Nothing good comes from sterile and pure.
The best things in life spring up from manure.

Thought Balloon

Fragile, floaty as a

balloon of helium or a soap bubble

wafting on thermals to land. Who knows where?

A cloudy thought, changing each moment, unfixed

amorphous, enigmatic, will o'the wisp whispering

in the corner of my mind and very soon to be lost.

Unformed thought full of wonder and wandering

untrammelled by need to conform flies free.

Ink and paper traps wait and watch.

Mouths intent on speech.

Capture captivating

controlled

caught

told.

No

more

free

but

here

to

hold.

Little Jimmy and the Sweet Corn of Doom or to split infinitives and beyond

Don't be afraid Little Jimmy
the Giant is stuck in the tin.
Canner Man used his powers
to safely trap him in.

But the Giant's evil henchman
hatched a plan with glee
to fool folk the tin just holds corn
so they'll open it and set him free.

Among the millions of tins of corn
there's one that holds our foe.
Will it be the tin that gets opened for your meal?
There's only one way to know.

For James Lollobrigida

In every breath as always potential for disaster

Life in its strongest form
constantly mutating
altering its rDNA
by self replicating.
So we go on oblivious
to the battle always raging,
fought by our immune system
and its constant macrophaging.

But even a biovirus
cannot hide from fame.
The WHO
just picks on one
to give a snappy name.

Pronounces it 'pandemic'
stirs up panic and fear,
to create a celebrity virus,
that we can't 'get out of here'.

So we are petri-fied
with face masks that don't work,
mistrusting our immune response
to the viruses that lurk.
And mass hysteria thrives
on the mis-truths being stated,
fed and kept alive
and self replicated.

A Question of Pants!!

My pants are white,
my pants are yellow,
my pants are blue,
my pants are red.

Some have cartoons on them
of Bart or Homer,
sometimes I wear them
on my head.

My pants are trendy boxer shorts,
I wear them on the beach
and cover them in sand.

My pants are cool
and cotton comfy,
I wear them on the outside
to be like superman.

But there's this problem with my pants
which really gets me down.
Why don't the shops sell them in brown?

The Hero Party

Celebration.
Nobody came
to light your candles,
blow out their flames.

It takes a strength
of heart and mind
to face disappointment
leave it behind.

You're my hero
I stand in awe
of the man you've become
a child no more.

For Alister.

Grown Ups

'What does grown-up feel like?'
I asked my dear Mama.
'Not now dear I'm busy
please go and ask Papa.'

'What is it like to be grown-up
Papa? Oh do tell me!'
'Go and ask your grandma
she should know she's sixty-three.'

'Grandma can you tell me
what being grown-up is like?'
'You'll find out soon enough child.
Be off and ride your bike.'

Here I am at 47 still without a clue.
I don't feel like a grown-up yet, do you?

For Menne - always young at heart.

Papa's Poem

A long time ago you held my hand
as we walked
through the bears and monsters.

You taught me to face
the scary things
and make them back down.

I looked up into your bearded face
full of crinkly smiles and knowing.
The smell of cigars, linen,
lint and machine oil lingering.

I thought you knew how to do magic,
how to disappear.
I searched through the rooms of the bungalow
sniffing the air for your smell and listening very hard
in case you gave yourself away.

I know now that you had gone to the shop.
I waited and waited
for you to reappear – and you always did.

You have found out how to do magic and really disappear.
I shouldn't be afraid any more now than I was then
but just sniff the air sometimes
and listen very hard in case it's you I hear.
Not gone very far away and hiding somewhere near.

Entente Cordiale

When my French father first came to Britain
He was scared to laugh at a joke.
For although he knew the British
were a very dignified folk,
he had expected to fit in
& live happily ever after
until he read the headline
'Jailed 10 years for mans laughter.'

Land of my Mothers

Where have you gone to land of my past,
where are your days so bright?

Where are the hours of warm content
spent safe asleep at night?

Where are the strong authorities
kindly and concerned?

Where are the staid academies
where earnest children learned?

Where are the sparkling hospitals
with nurses crisp and clean?

Where have you gone to land of my past,
as if you had never been?

For Tim Rees who lives there still.

Mother and the Monkey

My mother had a monkey,
she never said what sort,
it was when she lived in India
and came from the wild not bought.

It was supposed to be a tame one
and with it she played,
until it turned and bit her,
then she got afraid.

Grandma asked a servant
to take the monkey away
because it had bitten her daughter
and she didn't want to play.

My mum was still interested
in the monkey though it was vicious,
so she asked the servant how it was
and the servant said
'Delicious!'

For my mother – who else?

Mad Dog and Englishman

Heart thumping, terror rising, focussed clarity.
There is no doubt or time to ponder.
Only action lies ahead.

A breath to
        steady trembling weakness.

A microsecond to
        plan not hesitate.

This must work and instinct knows
the rightness of your next intent.

But as you
        face the enemy
a mad dog
        leaps and bares its teeth.

Panic is its only thought.

Even you who sought to help must
        fight,
not only foe but friend, to
        stand.

Alone as always at the end.

Tea-Pot of Trouble

There was a family of gnomes
who loved drinking tea.
Slurping those antioxidants
filled them with tannin and glee.

But they all shared a stubbourness gene
that often caused them trouble,
and arguing about who should make the tea
made that problem double.

So they had a family meeting
and by the time they had adjourned
they'd decided the best way forward
was they should all take turns.

They didn't write down a rota,
they memorised instead,
but they all had dreadful memories.
You can tell there'll be trouble ahead.

Now this family of gnomes was made up
of Father Gnome and Mother
and Gloria their teenage daughter gnome
that's three - there was no other.

Gloria had a boyfriend gnome
who rode a motorbike,
he didn't figure in the tea making plans
and his name was Scruffy Mike.

Well as could have been expected
the rota went to pot,
whose turn it was to make the tea
was very soon forgot.

The argument raged on and on,
needing a solution found.
Said Dad, "Okay listen here's the plan,
no-one must make a sound.

The first gnome who makes a noise
will have to make the tea.
But I'm saying now, I'm promising
that gnome will not be me."

So it was agreed and there they sat quiet as you'd like,
it was easy to hear Gloria's boyfriend arrive
outside on his motorbike.

In came Scruffy Mike to see his Gloria Gnome
and found the entire family sitting silently at home.

"Hello Gloria!" Mike said to her
but his girlfriend made no reply.
Mike repeated, "Hello Gloria!"
and looked her in the eye.

She met his gaze, said not a word
and his temper began to heat.
Mike turned to Mother Gnome
with a look that was not too sweet.

"Mother Gnome, why is Gloria ignoring me today?"
Mother Gnome smiled at Scruffy Mike
but nothing would she say.

"What the bleep is going on?"
Mike asked Father with a curse.
But Father Gnome did not reply,
Mike's temper just got worse.

"Right," said Mike.
"Here's what I'll do to make you speak to me,
I'll have my way with your daughter Gnome,
on this table set for tea."

Father Gnome's mouth went into a line.
Mother Gnome's mouth went thin.
Gloria looked a bit concerned,
but none of them would give in.

No matter the provocation,
how bad it came to be,
those stubborn gnomes would make no sound,
or they'd have to make the tea.

Mike carried out his promise
or more accurately his threat,
The Gnomes all looked extremely cross
but they weren't making noises yet.

By now Mike was in a fury,
his temper knew no bounds,
He repeated his threat now for Mother Gnome.
Still none of them made a sound.

Then it was done and Mother Gnome and Gloria
were put back in their chairs,
looking a bit dishevelled
with slightly mussed up hair.

Mike decided he was giving up
and leaving perhaps for good,
so he went off to start his motorbike
to ride back to his home in the wood.

But he slipped as he tried to kick start the bike
and the pain he felt was keen,
he had a cut on his shin so went back
to ask for some Vaseline.

Father Gnome heard Scruffy Mike's request
added one and one - got three.
Decided that enough was enough and said,
"I'll make the tea!"

I Quit

If persevering means letting them win;

I quit.

If taking their shit means not giving in;

I quit.

If denying what's right means
I might win the glitter.
I'd rather lose now and
be known as a quitter.

So just in case I'm not being clear,
I'll say it loud enough so you can hear;

I Quit!

Dog Day Afternoon

The priest was taking confession
to absolve in Jesus' name,
when in came, let's call him, Mr X,
to protect him from his shame.

He had some terrible sins to confess,
many a sordid crime,
he carnally enjoyed canines
and he did it all the time.

The priest was quite beside himself,
he got into a frightful lather,
said, 'Mother of God how low can you stoop?'
To be told, 'A corgi Father.'

Gone.

The Person who said "Yes" to Spam

I have a penis so large
I can't get out the door.
So many women want me
that although it's huge it's sore.

I've taken so much Viagra
I'm permanently aroused,
and drilled through so many walls
I have to be rehoused.

I wear a Rolex watch so good
you can't tell that it's fake.
I've lost a ton of weight
on a brand new diet shake.

I've found a part time job
that I can do from home.
But I don't need it as I've got millions
according to Mr N'Gome.

All I needed to do was send him a hundred quid,
'cos the authorities' palms needed greasing
and so that's what I did.

It was the very last of my social security check,
but soon I'll be stinking rich
and therefore 'what the heck?'

But having a very large penis,
and all these women chasing,
is more than a little embarrassing,
it's something I shouldn't be facing.

When I get my Nigerian millions
I'll have to give surgery a whirl,
so I can get back to normal after all I am a girl.

For Ron Price.

Lessons will be learned

Lessons will be learned.

Lessons will be learned?

Innocents are stabbed and raped,

children have been burned.

Yet still towards a blackboard

the authorities are turned.

They have no time to heed us;

our cries to them are spurned.

They just repeat the mantra chalked there:

Lessons will be learned

In memory of Fiona & Frankie Pilkington RIP.

A Prickly Problem

Sleeps curled up in duvet nest,
knees against his hairy chest
Prickly bristles on his chin,
shave them off and they grow again.

Weird weird Dad.

'Watch the traffic!' is what he shouts
every time we venture out.
Prickly bristles in the sink ,
ruining soap and on everything.

Weird weird Dad.

Suddenly it hit me,
   the truth was crystal clear,
      bristles, lack of energy in winter,
         that whole 'road crossing' fear.

The sad result of science
   playing a cruel joke.
      My Dad - a cross between a hedgehog
         and an ordinary sort of bloke!

Now what to do about Tony
   my older teenage brother?
      Should I tell him straight away
         or discuss it with my mother?

He thinks he has no problems
as long as his team is winning.
But yesterday on his spotty chin
was the hint of bristles beginning!

Eating toast and drinking tea,
things seem as they ought to be.
Bristles shaved its not so bad
he's all I've known and all I've had.

Weird weird Dad.

Poising I Be

Am I what I think?
Am I what you see?
Am I anything at all?
Am I even me?

"I think therefore I am,"
a philosopher once said.
"But if I don't think am I not?"
keeps circling in my head.

And what to think of you?
You're 'me' inside your mind.
But if everyone is 'me'
why is 'me' so rarely kind?

I do not want to think.
Thinking makes me sad.
So I'm poising at the brink
to dive neatly into mad.

Mad is nice and safe
it's where I want to be.
Curled up within my cosy shell
content unthinkingly.

Halfway round the bend

Halfway round the bend
is a place where I fit.
There isn't any other place
quite like it.
It's not plainly bonkers
it's not really sane,
but it is the spot where
I've got my brain.

Halfway round the bend
isn't bad it isn't good.
I wouldn't have it otherwise
even if I could.
I'm never in the doldrums
and never feel tip-top.
I'm always somewhere in between
and that is where I stop.

Halfway round the bend
is a jolly place to be.
There are always lots of other folk
here with me.
So if you're the sort of person who
reads novels from the end
You're probably my cup of tea,
and halfway round the bend.

For Pierre Van Rooyen - definitely my cup of tea.

Torreilles

There is a place,

    the water ripples,
    hopping insects flit past.
    The sudden dip of the sand
    as it slips into the sea.

Light ebbs gently,

    darkness velvet soft
    stitched with starlight sequins,
    the wind sings and caresses me.

In the morning,

    when the sun awakes,
    a hazy cloud of heat
    almost solid - appears.

I would,

    swim in the water,
    dance on the sand,
    float on the wind,

Never to leave
that place.

The World on its Head

Sometimes the world stands on its head.
You would think that the seas would slosh about
that it would at the very least
give people a bit of a headache,
but everything goes on as normal instead.

Sometimes the world starts spinning the other way.
You would think that physics demands
that buildings would topple
that someone would notice this phenomenon,
but everyone just carries on with their day.

When a single dog howls its fears to the moon
and the birds just stop in silent hush,
it happens again, and again and again
but people don't notice it in their rush.

Sometimes the world stands on its head.
Sometimes the world spins the other way.
Sometimes funny is simply sad,
and all we can do is play.

A Couple of Haiku

I

An Autumn earthquake.
The trees tremble dropping leaves
but their roots hold firm.

II

Winter hurricane.
Trees uprooted crash to earth
but grass merely bends.

For Helen Kennedy.

Nu Labour Christmas Carol
(to the tune of Ding Dong Merrily on High)

Ding dongs merrily on high
with coins in wallets clinking.
The ding dongs never even try
to tax their brains with thinking.

With no sense prevailing,
social workers failing,
civil servants mailing secret lists,
The UK's finally sinking.

'Elf & Safety' rule our lives
without them we'd be doing
things like juggling with knives
followed by years of suing -

councils not performing,
drunken yobboes storming
through our previously quiet lands,
we know that trouble's brewing.

Don't stop a bobby for the time
because he's busy dogging.
He's oblivious to crime
he's having more fun snogging.

The streets are cold and dirty,
too risky past 5.30,
if there's a murder simply phone it in
they'll note it in call logging.

Santa flying in his sleigh
with gifts for friends and neighbours,
decides he's calling it a day
he's been bitten by a dog named Sabre.

The presents undelivered,
kiddies lips aquiver,
this is Christmas in the great UK.
Many thanks Nu Labour.

For Daily Mail readers everywhere.

De Problem with De-Fooing

Maybe we didn't shout enough
to wound his gentle senses?

But something somewhere failed
to cause enough intense offences.

And now we have the credit crunch
and money is very tight.

It costs a lot to support our son
and continue doing right.

He likes us and our company
and likes the food I cook,

I've dropped some hints and even
sent him *here to have a look.

I've tried ignoring his welfare,
this demanding fruit of my womb.

But the little git won't **DEFOO** us,
so we can't rent out his room.

*http://www.freedomainradio.com

DEFOOing is when someone decides to separate from their
Family **O**f **O**rigin. It used to be called disowning, but was more
commonly a top down approach in which aggrieved senior
family members would cast those out of favour into the cold cold
snow, never to be mentioned again and to have their name
struck from the family bible.
These days it has been re-invented and the youngsters are doing
before done to, and in some cases even where it wasn't going to
be done to.

Call me 'Home'

I went into the world and it was cold.
They weren't my kind of people,
I was not theirs.
Then you called me
       'Home.'

We close our eyes
       hear
       the sounds we make
       feel
       our bodies breathing
       know
       we are safe.

You return each day from the place
       outside.

The attacks made on you forgotten
       our child laughs and plays for you,

and my greatest achievement is:

       I am 'Home.'

For Andy.

Happy Anniversary Darling – 20 years and never a cross word spoken, but many snarled shouted and screamed

So shall I howl?
Would it break the mood that clings to us enshrouding?
Do you doubt it?
As always you encompass that which smothers hope.
Shall I howl?
I ask again - will answers be forthcoming?
Will we speak?
Of course we won't - silence claims its victory.

The tea cup
warm and heavy beside a glinting spoon.
The marmalade jar,
stuck to the saucer whilst a fly sneaks toward it
from the sunlit window.

You never remember to close the insect screen,
and why can't you keep your mouth closed when you chew?
Do you hate me sometimes as much as I hate you?

For married couples everywhere.

Here Today, Gone Tomorrow

Here and now.
The magpie swoops.
The blackbird gathers
dried grass from the new mown lawn
while enemies circle.
Coughing from lungs poisoned by evil
under a promise-filled blue sky.

The sea calls.
Gulls sing in pain.
The clouds wincing
to hear their heart-torn noise
yet still we struggle.
Fighting the endless insanities
under siege - never giving in.

To sail away.
To wander free.
To leave the filthiness behind.

Lost in clean purity.
Small in the bigness.
Oblivious and empty of all that defiles.

Waiting for a peace and quiet
that will take us in
and swallow us whole.
Forever.

For Justin.

Father's Day

I hate you! I really really hate you!

I say it all the time,

you drive me mad,

bloody Dad.

Is it such a crime to leave my bedroom in a tip

and make my mother cry?

You don't try to understand me

you just roll your eyes and sigh.

You make me eat, and make me wash

you're such a control freak.

But I'll have the last laugh on you both

I'm moving out next week.

Summer anticipated

Sitting on the sun-kissed balcony,
hot air all around.
Cicadas buzzing, lavender in flower,
green olives dripping from the trees.

A holiday plane flies over head,
carrying eager tourists.
Tavernas bustling, calamari sizzling,
beaches rowed with sunbeds and sunbrellas.

The sea twelve blues all sparkling,
fish glinting in the light.
Afternoon boats packed with families
diving for squid with spears and snorkels.

I'm waiting for that to come again,
watching the Spring return.
Crocuses, Daisies, and other yellow flowers
promise me it won't be long.

I drink my ouzo quietly, wait, and yearn.

For Marie Elena – a kind, valued web friend and poet.

Government Advice for Summer in the UK

It's getting warm in Britain
so please try and take care.
It's time to put your feet on ice
and freeze your underwear.

You can't leave your windows open
or the burglars might get in.
You can't go out to feel the breeze
in case you burn your skin.

Be careful with your children,
the sun will fry them crispy.
Their eyes will boil in their sockets
and their hair will go all wispy.

But the wonderful GOVERNMENT
will save you, you need have no fear,
they've done their research and found out
this happens every year!

They've put together useful hints
to help you to survive.
Thank God and bless them for it,
else how could you stay alive?

For staying in the shade
and drinking lots to rehydrate
are ideas so fiendishly clever
you'd need brains like William Gates.

So sing and dance
(but not too much because you'll get too hot)
and praise the heaven that sent you
the government you've got.

Love or 'In love'?

Love is a workaday emotion
'In love' is a strange conceit.
Love means sacrifice for others,
'In love' means you think they're sweet.

Love is practical and caring.
'In love' likes a scene or two.
Love will enter compromise.
'In love' wants to conquer you.

Love is gentle and supportive.
'In love' says, "You must love me".
Love says, "I want what makes you happy."
'In love' says, "That cannot be."

Love says, "I'll be here forever."
'In love' says, "Things aren't the same."
Love says, "We can work things out."
'In love' says, "You are to blame."

Love might not be as exciting
though it has its highs.
'In love' is a false emotion
based on pretty lies.

For Stubsy.

Nonsense Poem

The invincible victim raised his head
declaring "I'm a trifle dead."
"I'll be a little more tomorrow,"
and his nostrils quivered in his sorrow.

Tears trickling down his merry face
collected in a special place
betwixt his chin and bottom lip
and formed a huge and trembling drip.

The moisture now began to stream.
His sadness came in squeaks and screams.
His special place began to pour
and drowned a beetle on the floor.

For Ian Thorpe who helped give me confidence in my poetry.

Suffer little children...

"Always hold on tight to nurse for fear of finding something worse."

I used to love that poem, it warned but in a cosy way,
for children were the charmed ones protected in a rosy glow
of love and strawberry jam.

Older now I am with heart weary knowledge
to ache my bones. I know the giant exists
and truly grinds wherever he can.

Children are no longer safe, if indeed they ever were.
Chocolate spread hides evil deeds and slipping from a father's
grasp can end with intracranial bleeds.

I could list so many names innocents all
but I believe they matter more than being known for how they
died and all their suffering gone before.

A tiny insignificant thing - the wince that comes now with that
verse, my feelings less than anything for they have suffered
something worse.

The poem misquoted refers to 'Jim' from Hilaire Belloc's
Cautionary Tales 1920

Warn Parenting

Where to begin, oh where to begin,
the story of parents Mair and Gwyn?

They started out with love and laughter,
but went on to live snappily ever after.

To see it with outsider's eyes
they should have tried to compromise.

But from the day that they were wed
they were pitted head to head.

Neither one capitulating
finding it first quite stimulating.

Sniping and backbiting seemed a game,
at least until the children came.

Discouraging words were often spoken.
Hearts and promises often broken.

The children's needs were simply lost.
Parents heedless of the final cost.

If they meant at all then they meant well,
they didn't intend this bickering hell.

How to mend it, Father, Mother,
when all you do is blame each other?

Carnaval

Last year cold kiss
frost on face.
Black bin-liner sea
rolling the bay.

Fireworks gone.
Explosions done
We tied the boat
against the quay.

This year we'll take the car
in daylight's shine.
This time hold hands.
Keep hold.
Keep you.
Hold mine.

Cauliflower soup c'est delicieux

The humble cauliflower
is often overlooked,
it can be found extremely bland
served plain and overcooked.

Yet years ago I tasted soup
when in the South of France.
I asked for the recipe of what they called potage
but they said, "Pas de chance."

It took me years of trying
to reproduce that soup.
I tried a gazillion recipes
and jumped through culinary hoops.

Then inspiration hit me
and I used the blanc chouffleur
chucked it in the pressure cooker
for dix minuits not un heure.

Eventually added les ognions,
et a couple pommes de terres
plus three small cloves of garlic
I was very nearly there.

A knob of butter added et dill
to give je ne sais quoi.
Some salt and a bit of pepper
and je me dit, "Voila!"

But the tres tres secret thing
that I worked out yesterday
was to use the bit of the cauli
that I usually throw away.

When I used the curds the texture
was grainy and not 'just so.'
Yesterday I only used leaves and stalk,
and that's the way to go.

So serve a soup so delicious
it makes your diners weep,
and tastes as if you spent a fortune on it
though you know it was very cheap.

Tell them it's a secret recipe
from the South of France.
If they ask you to reveal it shrug and tell them,
"Pas de chance."

For Amit who liked this so much he 'stole' it.

Ode to a Greek Taxi Driver

The peace and quiet is very nice,
with echoes from the past.
But what eclipses all of this is

driving very fast
on narrow roads
with eyes tight shut,
trying not to weep
at views of beauty laid before them.

I'd rather be a sheep.
Standing still,
relaxed serene
feet firmly where they've always been.

Not hurtling
round the hair pin bends,
whilst praying for safe journey's end.

Finding home

Subtle as breath, cirrus gentle...

whispering softness of gossamer steel

waking memories long forgotten,

rock in blood and sea soul found.

More than a mother, father, children.

Deeper than friendship stronger than love.

Inexorable instinct denial negated.

Gut recognition – this is home ground.

Snooze and you lose

I have a very long list
of things I want to do,
then another twice as long
compiled by 'you know who.'

It tells me of the things
I must accomplish every day,
tasks I am 'asked' to complete
if I'm to get my pay.

Alas I work from home
and my bed is warm like heaven.
Too many days I find it
hard to rise before eleven.

There are so many dreams in store
I have no need of sheep.
I have dream miles to go a dream horse to ride
and dream promises to keep.

If I carry on like this
I will lose my job for sure.
The alarm clock can't compete
with my somnaudient nasal roar.

So the list of things I want to do
stays locked up in my heart,
and at the top is number one -
Get up and make a start!

Only fair to acknowledge the line from "Stopping by Woods on a
Snowy Evening" by Robert Frost which I 'adapted' for this
poem.

I took my love

I took my love to a mountain top
where the world lay under us.

Swooping between the sky and the sea
an eagle,
then three
calling to each other in the chilly mist.

I took my love to an ocean bed
where the sea flowed over us.

Looking upwards we could see turtles
and dolphins
swimming silhouetted against the bright warm sun.

I took my love to a darkened place
where the world could not reach us.

Sight, sound, touch, smell, taste
no longer held real meaning.
All there was,was our love.
It was enough.

For Emma and Stuart – may their love always be enough.

Mr BadShock

Mr BadShock crashes in.
Black bristles on his crumpled chin
a million frown lines on his face.
He screams at us to 'Sit In Place!'

Whisper low if you dare
his ears pick sound up everywhere.
'Shut Up Child!' is his battle cry,
a pen the missile he lets fly.

Mr BadShock frightens me
and everybody in 4B.
Our only hope and deep desire
Is that he's planning to retire.

Love all

After the blood and bruises,
he cries in her lap and says,
"It's only because I love you so much."
Because she loves him she stays.

My Funny Valentine

It's traditional on the day of St Valentine
to declare one's romantic feelings
in poem and rhyme,
and after 20 years of marriage to you,
I thought it was time
for me so to do.

My love is strong
and never ending,
passionate
and yet befriending.
I see faults as perfection
and cherish every quirk.
Problem is it's not you,
but a woman at work.

Now I've Grown

My heart won't smile, my soul won't sing.
My dreams and faith have taken wing.
I've learned the lessons I was shown.

I was a child - but now I've grown.

You showed that truths were only lies,
that one who fails is one who tries.
I dried my tears and stood alone.

I was a child - but now I've grown.

All things come to those who take.
If you don't care - then you can't break.
You start and end this life alone.

I was a child - but now I've grown.

I once had hopes.
I once had dreams.
Believed in love
and other things.

You turned my heart into a stone.
I once had hope - but now I've grown.

I can't forgive, my will won't bend.
I'm no-one's love, I'm no-one's friend.
I've taken all that I was thrown.

I was a child.
But now I've grown.

You can hear this song performed at this web address:
http://poems-2-share.blog.co.uk/2009/07/15/now-i-ve-grown-6518268/

What's in a name?

There was a woman
didn't live in a shoe
but a council apartment,
she might live near you.

Her children were named
in the hope one day
celebrity riches
would come their way.

So she chose their names
to help them stand out.
Didn't know what they meant
and at meal times she'd shout -

"Food's ready, Sestina,
Salmonella, Vagina,
Colonic, Ebola,
hurry up Spirulina!

Get it while it's hot
Gonnorrhea
you too Escherischa,
Candida, Chlamydia
and you Analfissure."

Proudly at table
she gazed at her brood,
future stars of TV,
gobbling their food.

For Sue – who knows this is (almost) true.

The games you play

Why are you so full?

Spilling over, gushing
cold malevolence,
drowning my soul.

Why am I empty?

Nothing - no one, no where
to hide and stay safe
and protected.

How can hurting me
be so intoxicating,
so tempting?

There is no answer.

Nothing - no where, no one
explanation
for your actions.

I hide, I wait, I pray
knowing it will not go away.

Money can't buy you love

I can't promise salvation
that isn't my domain,
or luck everlasting
or freedom from pain.

I can't help you find true love
though you are a millionaire,
or help you lose weight
or save your hair.

But if being super-rich
is making you sad
I have an idea
that isn't half bad.

Here's how I can help you
escape and be free.
Just give all your money to me!

Go on, you know you want to.

For Barbara Young who shares my sense of humour.

Yellow

"Stay inside!
Lock your door!
Don't do that!"

I shout at the stupid girl
wandering down the stairs at dead of night.

No power, the phone lines are down
but she heard a noise outside
so is determined to investigate.

Can't she tell from the music she's doomed?

"She is such an idiot," I mutter
from behind my cushion.

NEVER DO THE THINGS YOU SHOULD NEVER DO!!!!!!!!!!

She came on Twitter in a mood so bitter
that she said things she wished she hadn't.

Then her husband quit her for the baby sitter
leaving her not so much bitter as saddened.

Giving *TMI on the internet is never a good idea
the traces left are indelible and impossible to clear.

It's something we should never do,
like keeping tin tacks in your shoe
or filling your windscreen washer with glue
or admitting you like the smell of poo.

Unless you want us to remember you
as the person who did things they should never do
then please remember what I'm telling you -

NEVER DO THE THINGS YOU SHOULD NEVER DO.

*TMI = Too Much Information

For Victoria Twead who never did any of these things.

Michele Brenton born and brought up in Swansea, South Wales now lives on the Greek island of Kefalonia.

Any questions?
Visit me on the internet:

at my poetry blogs

http://poetry4fun.blog.co.uk

http://poems-2-share.blog.co.uk

http://TheAlternativePoetry.blog.co.uk

on Twitter

@banana_the_poet